Let's go!

Baby loves books.

THE ORIGINAL INDESTRUCTIBLES®

Chew Proof • Rip Proof • Nontoxic • 100% Washable

BABY LOVES THE LIBRARY

MILLIONS OF COPIES SOLD!

GRACE HABIB

Baby loves the library.

Let's pick
one to read.

Baby loves storytime.

Let's gather
and listen.

Baby loves
borrowing books.

Let's use
our library card!

Baby loves reading books
at home together.

Let's go back tomorrow!

THE ORIGINAL INDESTRUCTIBLES®

For ages 0 and up!

Books babies can really sink their gums into!

Books! Storytime!
Babies love everything about the library.

Spend the afternoon exploring the shelves in a book that's INDESTRUCTIBLE.

DEAR PARENTS: INDESTRUCTIBLES are built for the way babies "read": with their hands and mouths. INDESTRUCTIBLES won't rip or tear and are 100% washable. They're made for baby to hold, grab, chew, pull, and bend.

CHEW ALL THESE AND MORE!

$5.99 US / $7.99 Can.
ISBN 978-1-5235-3497-5
9 781523 534975 50599

 Library of Congress Cataloging-in-Publication Data is available. Workman Kids is an imprint of Workman Publishing, a division of Hachette Book Group, Inc. The Workman name and logo are registered trademarks of Hachette Book Group, Inc.

Distributed in the United Kingdom by Hachette UK Ltd., Carmelite House, 50 Victoria Embankment, London EC4Y 0DZ. Distributed in Europe by Hachette Livre, 58 rue Jean Bleuzen, 92 178 Vanves Cedex, France. Contact special.markets@hbgusa.com regarding special discounts for bulk purchases.

All INDESTRUCTIBLES books have been safety-tested and meet or exceed ASTM-F963 and CPSIA guidelines. INDESTRUCTIBLES is a registered trademark of Indestructibles, LLC.

First Edition December 2025 | 10 9 8 7 6 5 4 3 2 1
Printed in Shenzhen, China 10/25 | IMFP

WORKMAN PUBLISHING • Hachette Book Group, Inc., 1290 Avenue of the Americas, New York, NY 10104 • indestructiblesinc.com